Helga's Corner

Musings about German
Language and Culture

by

Helga von Schweinitz

Für Donovan Venuto.

Viel Spaß beim Lesen!

Helga von Schweinitz

6. Juni, 2013

Dedicated to:

Bettina and Christopher

The articles appeared originally in the *Schulhaus Reporter* in a regular column called "Helga's Corner" which is published six times a year by the German Free School Guild, a committe of the German-Texan Heritage Society, headquartered in Austin, Texas.
However, some of the articles were edited by the author to match the format of this book.

Table of Contents

SAUERKRAUT

What do you call a mad German? A sour kraut. Wash your mouth.

The Chinese developed a way to marinate white cabbage and invented what became popular in Germany as "*Sauerkraut*". *Kraut* can mean cabbage but it can also refer to other vegetables and especially to herbs. Kitchen herbs are *Küchenkräuter* or *Suppenkräuter*. Medicinal herbs are healing herbs, *Heilkräuter*.

Plural of *das Kraut* is *die Kräuter*. Many a household has a *Kräutergarten*, a herb garden just like many German pioneers had in America.

A popular part of the German line of beverages are the many types of tea (*Tee*) made of herbs (*Kräutertee*). While traveling in Germany you should try them. The most common *Tees* are *Pfefferminztee* to calm you down, and *Kamillentee* against indigestion. In a *Reformhaus* (a health food store) they have a *Tee* for whatever ails you, and many Germans prefer to cure themselves with a *Tee* rather than *Pillen* (pills).

What do you call a weed? *Ein Unkraut.*

Gegen Dummheit ist kein Kraut gewachsen.

❋❋❋

There's no herb that cures stupidity.

SCHNAPS

Even if you don't care to drink it, you should know the word: *der Schnaps*. It is the generic German word for hard liquor distilled from berries, grain, flowers, herbs or other basics. It comes with many names like *Aquavit, Steinhäger, Enzian, Wacholder, Korn, Ratzeputz...*

To drink a *Schnaps (einen Schnaps trinken)* is woven into the fabric of German culture. A host may offer you *ein Schnäpschen (*form of endearment*)* as a welcoming gesture. In a restaurant a new friend might ask you to come to the bar with him to seal the new friendship with a *Schnaps*. It can be part of the ritual when somebody offers you to call him the familiar *du* instead of the formal *Sie*. You then drink to brotherhood, *Bruderschaft trinken*.

There are many words with *Schnaps* in them, the most common one is *die Schnapsidee,* which is an idea that is not yet well thought through, or a hare-brained scheme.

My grandmother's *Schnaps,* which she concocted secretly in our basement right after WW II in Germany, was highly valued by American GIs who had their liquor rationed. They came in the dark of night, loaded with bread, Spry, corned beef and other badly needed food stuff in exchange for "Oma's tea". She had acquired the necessary skills in Milwaukee where she had lived during prohibition. It saved us children from going to bed hungry too often.

Here's to you, Oma! *Prost!*

Über Geschmack läßt sich streiten.

❦❦❦

One can argue about taste.

DIE HOSE

Hose (ho-ze) is the two-syllable German word for an item no Amecican should have to go without: pants, trousers, knickers, panties, briefs, etc..

Bavarians usually use the word in the plural: *Hosen.* All Bavarians, as the world knows, wear a special kind of *Hosen: die Lederhosen* (leatherpants). Underneath they wear (I suspect) *Unterhosen* (underpants).

If you wear undies made of cotton, you are wearing *Baumwollunterhosen.*

What we call "pantyhose" (panty-stockings), Germans call *Strumpfhose* (stocking-pants).

For skiing one sports *die Skihose,* for watersports *die Badehose* and, as sweatpants, *die Trainingshose.*

Some men secure their trousers with *Hosenträger* (suspenders), and when their fly is open, you should avoid looking at their *Hosenschlitz.*

Of the woman who is the real man of the house, it is said: *"Sie hat die Hosen an."*

Die Hose - don't leave your home without it.

**Wer andern eine Grube gräbt,
fällt selbst hinein.**

*He who digs a trap for others
falls into it himself.*

SKAT

SKAT (pronounced skaht) is a game played by many Germans. It is a card game (*Kartenspiel*) for three players (*drei Spieler*). Each game starts with some bidding (*reizen*), and the highest bidder plays against the other two, but just for that hand. On many an evening two guys decide to play *Skat*, and the proverbial search for "The Third Man" (*der dritte Mann*) begins.

Although German is used with a sprinkling of French when playing *Skat*, words take on a different meaning: *"aus dem Schneider", "der mauert", "Grand mit Vieren", "der Alte" "Durchmarsch"* are just a small sample of the *Skat*-language. Even behavior seems to be *Skat*-specific: bursts of excited, loud comments, slamming the fist holding a card on the table, playing into the wee hours of the morning, often in a pub, and then consuming a bowl of *Gulaschsuppe* or *Speck und Spiegeleier auf Roggenbrot* (bacon and fried eggs on rye) or some other sobering sustenance before going home.

I know of Skat tournaments and regular Skat club evenings in Amerika, but for a German in the old country his *Skatabend* is almost sacred.

Skat requires concentration and a good grasp of numbers. That's why I have never been good at it. I only play when certain men in my life are so desperately in need of a third man that they ask me - a woman who can barely count the cards in her hand - to be *"der dritte Mann"*.

Rom ist auch nicht an einem Tag erbaut worden.

Rome wasn't built in a day.

BURG VS. BERG

In English you pronounce ...burg just like you do ...berg.
That lead a certain Mr. Finkenburg to bark up the family tree of
the Finkenberg clan. Relying on sound rather than on correct
spelling, he found a great grandmother that wasn't his at all.
What confusion!

Burg means castle - like in *Hamburg* (pronounced
humboork); it can also refer to the community that developed
around the castle. *Berg* means mountain - like in *Heidelberg*
(pronounced hydelbarek); it can also be the name of the
settlement near or on that mountain. There is a town called
Wittenburg and another one called *Wittenberg*. Which one is the
"Luther town"?

For ...*burg* you can remember Fredericksburg in Texas
with its ooompahh bands. For the ...*berg* sound think of how
bare that nearby mountain is, the Enchanted Rock.

So many of you will always get it wrong, because if it can
go wrong, it will. After all, isn't that Merphy's law?

**Was Hänschen nicht lernt,
lernt Hans nimmermehr.**

You can't teach an old dog new tricks.

WAS IST DAS?

All too often someone says to me: „I know only three German words: *"Ich liebe dich"* (I love you).

That's really nice. But here is an opportunity for these linguists to increase their vocabulary without really trying:

The following words are all preceded by *"das"*, one of the German translations of "the". *Das* indicates that the noun (not the thing or person) is of the neuter gender.

das Haus	*das Sofa*	*das Auto*	*das Glas*
das Gras	*das Gas*	*das Radio*	*das Bier*
das Gold	*das Fräulein*	*das Ende*	

There are many words that are exactly like English words or close to it. You just have to look for them. Of course, they sound a little different in German.

Now say: „*Ich liebe das Sofa und das Bier.*"
„*Ich liebe das..............und das..............*"
„*Ich liebe das..............und das..............*"

Liebe macht erfinderisch.

❦❦❦

Love will find a way.

YOU MUST IT RIGHT GET

You must the word order right get! In 1949, John P. began to translate a paragraph of a German novel. He is still hung up on the first sentence, because he has yet to find the verb.

In German, words of a sentence follow a sequence which can be quite different from the word order of an English sentence.

If the verb of a simple clause consists of two words (as in „He has seen the light") the second part of the verb moves to the end of the sentence ("He has the light seen" = "*Er hat das Licht gesehen*".

Now, if you have seen the light, you will be able the following words in the right order to put: "*Meyer - Herr - mehr - Wasser - trinken - muss.* (Mr. Meyer must drink more water).

I want you a nice time wish. I hope that you enjoy German to learn.

Rache ist süß.

Revenge is sweet.

WHO IS WHERE?

Wer ist wo?

Most German question words (*Fragewörter*) are easy to learn:

was = what?
wann = when?
warum = why?
wieviel = how much?
wessen = whose?
wie = how?
wer = who?
wo = where?

"*Wo und wer?*" is easily mistaken to mean "Who and where?", although it means "Where and who?" Imagine your mother's face when you ask her "*Wer ist mein Vater?*", when all you want to know is where your father is at the moment.

Now take your *Kuli* (ballpoint pen) and fill in the blanks:

when= _____?   what=_____ ?
how=_____?   why =_____?
how much =_____?   who =_____?
whose =_____?   where =_____?

One question (*Frage*) that should always be asked and answered with accuracy when food poisoning breaks out: „Who ate what?"

In German, the language of philosophers, you should ask: "*Wann aß wer wo wessen was - und warum?*"

Man ist, was man ißt.

One is what one eats.

KNÖDEL ANYTIME

In spite of Pizza Huts and Burger Kings sprouting all over Germany, the country is still offering a great variety of dishes that we rarely find in America. One of the specialties is the dumpling (*der Knödel*, also called *der Kloß*).

Recipies change from region to region, but most *Knödel* are made from one of four basic ingredients: raw or boiled potatoes (*Kartoffelknödel*), yesterday's white bread (*Semmelknödel*), grits (*Griesknödel*) or meat (*Fleischknödel*). The famous *Leberknödelsuppe* is a soup with *Semmelknödel* which have liver *(Leber)* mixed in.

Kartoffelknödel and *Semmelknödel* have to be eaten with lots of gravy or saucy meats like Gulasch, or with juicy vegetables like a mild *Sauerkraut*. They can be enhanced by mixing in fried onions and bacon, croutons, caraway seeds, etc.. *Griesknödel* can be filled with prunes or other fruit and served in hot vanilla pudding (hmmhmmmmhmm!!)

One plump, bacon filled *Semmelknödel* in a bowl of broth at four in the morning when the party is over takes the edge off the hangover (*Kater*).

Just before my last trip to Germany my doctor told me to go on a diet. I picked the *Knödel-Diät* and was very happy with it.

Es ist nicht alles Gold was glänzt.

All that glitters is not gold.

NOBODY DIES

Nobody dies learning German. The word „*die*" is one of the many translations of „the". „*Die*" rhymes with „she", not with „shy".

Die indicates that a noun is of the feminine gender - remember: not the thing is necessarily feminine, only the word. the girl is *das* Mädchen.

Do you recognize these German words? (The lonesome e at the end of some of the nouns is pronounced like the a in „Have a nice day".)

> *die Rose   die Maus   die Banane   die Bibel*
> *die Hand   die Maschine   die Laus*
> *die Oma   die Katastrophe.*

Most nouns that end with an e after a consonant are of the feminine gender. *die Liebe, die Schokolade, die Tasse, die Garage, die Margarine.*

Almost all nouns with the following endings are feminine: *-ung (die Übung); -tät (die Universität); -ion (die Station); -ik (die Grammatik); -schaft (die Botschaft)*

Die Statistik sagt: when in doubt about *der, die* or *das,* use *die.*

Erst besinn's, dann beginn's!

Look before you leap.

DARE TO SAY *DER*

The German word „*der*" is another one of the many translations of the English „the". It rhymes somewhat with „dare" and is said to indicate the masculine gender of a noun. That does not mean that the item is masculine but that the word is "masculine".

der Finger	der Film	der Garten
der Mann	der Schuh	der Motor
der Idiot	der Arm	der Opa

You can guess that a noun might be masculine by considering the ending: *or (der Motor); us (der Kaktus); er (der Lehrer* - especially if the *er* is added to the stem of a verb: *lehren - der Lehrer; sprechen - der Sprecher).*

Here are a few verbs to practice with:
schreiben - der..................
lesen - der..............
hören - der.............

There are other rules, but they are too unreliable. However, you can always dare to say *der.*

21

Die Tat wirkt mächtiger als das Wort.

Actions speak louder than words.

SHOULD WE NEUTER THEM ALL?

The language of grammar has a major flaw: it uses the words feminine, masculine and neuter to describe the so-called gender of a noun. The origin of this practice may lie in prehistoric times, but for modern man it creates too much confusion.

Why is *der Tisch* (the table) "masculine" in German and "feminine" (la mesa) in Spanish? Why is there *die See* (the sea) and *der See* (the lake)? Why is *das Fräulein* (the unmarried woman) neuter? Why do you say: *Ich gehe in die Stadt. Ich komme aus der Stadt?*

We should remember that it is not the object that has a gender but the word for it, but who can keep all that in mind? In German you can simplify matters somewhat because you can make all nouns neuter, i. e. *das*-words. You simply add *-chen* or *-lein* or regional variations thereof like *-le* or *-li*. Let's neuter your mother: die Mutter - *das Mütterchen* or *das Mütterlein*, then let's neuter my brother etc....der Bruder - *das Brüderlein*, der Tisch - *das Tischlein*....

Although grammatically always correct, neuteralization is not always appropriate. Therefore I challenge you all to come up with new words to be used instead of "masculine", "feminine", "neuter" and "gender" in the language of grammar.

Please send suggestions to my attention.

Ein Unglück kommt selten allein.

When it rains it pours.

DER - DIE - DAS RAT

Some good advice from Helga: If you don't know when to use *das, die* or *der*, don't worry.   It's more important to use the right word following the *der, die* or *das*.

Our friend Anita travelled through Europe with a German cousin twice removed and admired the beaufiful Baroque *Kirschen* (cherries) instead of the *Kirchen* (churches) they were visiting.   She also told him that she wanted to spoil her *Koffer* (suitcase) with a hot bath.   She meant to spoil her *Körper* (body).

Since *der, die* and *das* can change to *dem, des, den, denen, dessen* and so forth - depending on their function in the sentence - some not so dumb folks use either always *die* or an unspecified *de*.

As a teacher of German I urge you to study the fine points of grammar, but until you have mastered them, don't hesitate to babble away in German anyhow.   But don't neglect to learn lots of vocabulary words so you don't offer your *Körper* to be searched instead of your *Koffer*.

Was nicht ist kann noch werden.

❦❦❦

Your day will come.

FANTASTISCH

Fantastisch! The German language is changing rapidly (*rapide*). Many of our English words with "'ph" are used with the same meaning in German, but in many cases the "ph" changed to "f" in recent years. The photographer is *der Fotograf*, the telephone is *das Telefon*, a phantastic idea is *eine fantastische Idee*, but a philosopher is still *ein Philosoph* - (as of this writing).

So, let's not take it too seriously right now. Let's be filosofical about it and ask ourselves, which words are now ph-words and which are f-words. Is it *Physik* or *Fysik*? Is it just a *Phase* or a *Fase* the Germans are going through? Is it a temporary *Phänomen* or *Fänomen*? I am a little phlabberghasted about it.

Just for the phun of it, look in the dictionary for words with "ph". Do they all look Greek to you? At the same time you'll be surprised at how much German you know.

Hilf dir selbst, so hilft dir Gott.

God helps those who help themselves.

DU, IHR, SIE - THOU, YOU

Thou don't have to ask yourself any longer whether to use *du, ihr,* or *Sie* for our English thou and you.

God, children, animals, family members, first name friends and any inanimate objects you might talk to are addressed with *du* (singular) or *ihr* (plural). *"Lieber Gott, du musst mir helfen."* (Dear God, you have to help me.)

Adults whom we call by their last name or whose name we don't even know or whom we address by their titles are *Sie*-persons (singular and plural). *"Herr Pastor, Sie müssen mir helfen."* (Pastor, you have to help me!)

The singular and plural *Sie*=you is always capitalized. It is actually the pronoun *sie*=they which is used as a polite way to address someone, a courtesy formerly reserved for kings and the likes. That's why *Sie*=you goes with the same verb form as *sie*=they. *Wo sind sie?* (Where are they)? and *Wo sind Sie?* (Where are you?)

Du is the old thou which God used when he gave the Ten Commandments to the English speaking world. But nowadays polite society addresses everybody with you (a variation of ye), actually as a plural entity which equals the German *ihr*=you all.

Translate this question: Who are you? (There are at least three answers).
Answers: *1. Wer bist du? 2. Wer seid ihr? 3. Wer sind Sie?*

Nach dem Essen sollst du ruh'n
oder tausend Schritte tun.

After eating rest a while
or take a walk for half a mile.

FRESSEN

Fressen, fraß, gefressen, er frisst.

Although your pooch has impeccable table manners, his eating is not called „*essen*" in German, but „*fressen*".

You don't say „*Der Hund isst*", you say „*Der Hund frisst*". *Der Mensch isst, das Tier frisst.*

When human animals eat too much or in a sloppy manner, we say "*sie fressen*". *Tante Frieda fraß wie ein Scheunendrescher* (Aunt Frieda ate like a threshing machine in a barn). *Sie war sehr dick.* (She was very fat).

Many Germans try to stick to a diet called „F.d.H." (eff-day-hah), which stands for „*Friss die Hälfte*" and means „eat only half as much as you want to". It works for my sisters.

Some all-you-can-eat restaurants are called „*Fress - Paradiese*". However, I have not seen any in Germany, only in the good old USA.

Remember: *Der Mensch ist was er isst...(*and *: was er frisst).*

Man muß die Feste feiern
wie sie fallen.

✧✦✧

You have to celebrate when you have
the opportunity.

IT'S *IN*

In German you have a great way to indicate that a person is of the feminine gender: you add "in".

> *der Professor* - *die Professorin* (the professor - the female professor);
> *der Lehrer* - *die Lehrerin*   (the teacher - the female teacher);
> *der Bäcker* - *die B*.............. (the baker - the female baker)

This is done mainly with professions, but also with nouns that are not actually an adjective turned into a noun:

> *der Nachbar* - *die Nachbarin* (the neighbor - the female neighbor)
> *der Freund* - *die Freundin* (the friend - the female friend, lady friend or not)

A note to genealogists: In some registries the "*in*" is even added to a woman's name:

Robert Müller und Luise Müllerin.

If you were told: "Your neighbor has an affair," wouldn't it be nice to know if its the he-neighbor who's having an affair or if she is the one?

*Sei freundlich gegen jederman,
dann sieht dich jeder freundlich an.*

*Be friendly towards everybody;
then everybody will look friendly at you.*

DONNERWETTER!

The so-called four letter words have more than four letters in German, of course. Take "*Donnerwetter*" which can express anger or surprise. The basic translation is "thunder weather".

Germans in predominantly catholic areas tend to swear in religious terms, from the acceptable "*Himmel*" (heaven) to the Holy Family.

In the more protestant northern regions, references to the digestive system and the animal world are preferred: A mean guy is a "*Schweinehund*" (a swine hound).

Words with a sexual meaning are not as commonly used in German for their shock effect as they are in English.

The first and often only German word some American GIs enjoy learning is what in English is a four letter word beginning with "sh". It is now widely used in Germany and hardly shocks anybody anymore. However, like in English, it is enough to sound out just the first "sh" sound without completing the word, but when you think in German, you have to realize that the "sh" sound has three letters in German: "*Sch...*"

Now, wasch your mouth *aus*!

Man soll den Tag nicht vor dem Abend loben.

Don't praise the day before evening.

A VISIT TO THE *UMLAUT*-GARDEN

"*Umlaut*" means "change in sound". If an a, o or u are topped by two dots (*ä, ö, ü*) their pronunciation is changed. It's difficult to practice sound in writing, but no matter how you pronounce it, in writing you can always replace the dots by placing an „*e*" behind the vowel. *Händel - Haendel, König - Koenig, Müller - Mueller.*

Many German immigrants made the change from an *Umlaut* with dots to adding the *e* to the vowel when they moved here. However, some dropped the Umlaut altogether, like the Schutze family in Austin, Texas, which used to be the *Schütze* family, although the part of the *Schütze* family that settled in San Antonio is now the Schuetze family.

Other families that immigrated with an *Umlaut*, like the Pörtner clan, first changed it to Poertner and then dropped the o, not the e. That spelling kept the sound of the original name, like Pertner. Some members of the present generation don't even know that there was an o involved five generations ago.

Genealogists beware!

Kommt Zeit, kommt Rat.

Time will tell.

A SIGHT AT NIGHT

Is the neighbor's light in sight at night? Many German words with *ch* have a similar word in English with a silent gh or an f-sounding gh.

acht = eight;   *rechts* and *richtig* = right;   *hoch* = high;
lachen = laugh;   *nichts* = naught;   *er dachte* = he thought.

Unfortunately, this relationship is not true for every *ch* (no matter how you pronounce it), but you can always give it a try:

Nacht =---------.
Macht =----------.
in Sicht =--- ----------.
Nachbar =-----------.
Schlachthaus 7 =------------------ ------.
Licht = ------------.
Winter brachte Eis und leichten Schnee = ----------------
--.

Kein Feuer, keine Kohle
Kann brennen so heiß,
Als heimliche Liebe,
Von der niemand nichts weiß.

No fire, no coal can burn as hot
As secret love of which no one knows naught.

LIEBE - IS IT LOVE?

Love --- In English we make it, we fall in it, and we give it the value of zero in a game of tennis when we start scoring with love - fifteen. We can't translate these expressions literally into German. Germans don't say *Wir machen Liebe.* When a German falls in love he says *Ich bin verliebt.* And a game of tennis begins with *null - fünfzehn.*

If you are a man and a lover, you are not a *Lieber,* you are a *Liebhaber.* You use *lieber* when you prefer one thing over another: *Ich esse Butter lieber als Margarine.*

Too often we chirp "I love you!" which is embarrassing to a German who is not used to our culture. The German *"Ich liebe dich!"* is more sincere, rather intimate.

Poets beware: Love rhymes with dove - a peaceful image. *Liebe* rhymes with *Triebe* (driving urges, strong desires): *Die süßesten Triebe beflügeln meine Liebe.* (The sweetest desires give wings to my love).

And *Meine wildesten Triebe sind meine Schokoladen-Liebe.* (The wildest urges make me eat chocolate).

41

Was man sät, das erntet man.

You reap what you sow.

PAMPERS

"We pamper Grandma five times a day," said our young German visitor. We had asked him to practice his English on us, and it soon became clear, that Germans had absorbed many English words, given them a different meaning thinking that they meant the same in both languages.

For us "Pamper" is a brand name of a disposable diaper. In Germany it now stands for any disposable diaper, and it is also a verb meaning to put a disposable diaper on a person (*Wir pampern Oma fünf mal am Tag*).

"Grandma has her own *handy*," said our visitor. "Handy what?" I asked. It turns out, that a *Handy* is a cell phone.

"Grandma eats a lot of Philadelphia strength cheese since her fall.." "What is strength cheese?" " In Germany we now have a cheese called *Kraft* which means "strength" in English." He was talking about Philadelphia cream cheese form Kraft.

"Grandma won't let my brother Max into her house since he turned *Republican*." Well, I know that a member of the German party of *Republikaner* is extremely right wing, a nationalist, so I had to describe American Republicans to him.

All that reminded me of a German ad for a vacuum cleaner (*Staubsauger* = dust sucker) which appeared in English which is so fashionable in advertising: "Nothing sucks like Electrolux".

Aller Segen kommt von oben.

***

All blessings come from above.

IT'S SO ADVERBIAL!

Some of us handle adverbs real good, others do so really well. In German we don't have a problem with adverbs because we use a basic adjective as an adverb, without adding an ending or switching to another word:

Let's take „*schön*" (beautiful): *Zur Weihnachtszeit ist unser Schulhaus schön dekoriert.* (At Christmas time our school house is beautifully decorated.)

Let's take „gut" (good*): Ein guter Motor läuft gut.* (A good motor runs well.)

Ist diese einfache Regel nicht einfach fantastisch? (Is this simple rule not simply phantastic?)

Manche von uns sprechen Deutsch sehr gut, andere nicht so gut. (Some of us speak German very well, others don't do so good.)

**Wer Arbeit kennt und sich nicht drückt,
der ist verrückt.**

**If you don't shirk wörk,
you are a jerk.**

AMUSINGLY DESCRIPTIVE

Some German words are so descriptive! You'll find a few of them in the left column and the proper English expressions for them on the right, but in the wrong order. Please, match the letters with the numbers:

1. *der Staubsauger* (dust sucker)   a. diarrhea
2. *die Glühbirne* (glow pear)   b. alarm clock
3. *der Wecker* (waker)   c. typewriter
4. *die Hochzeit* (high time)   d. honeymoon
5. *der Durchfall* (fall through)   e. wedding
6. *das Taschenbuch* (pocketbook)   f. secretly
7. *heimlich*   g. lightbulb
8. *die Flitterwochen* (tinsel weeks)   h. paperback
9. *die Schreibmaschine* (writing machine) i. bra
10. *BH („bay hah")* (bh)   j. vacuum cleaner

A little help: *BH* stands for *Büstenhalter* (bust holder). Don't tell anybody I used that word in my article.

These words make for delightful underholding *(Unterhaltung)* at a rooster tail party *(auf Deutsch: Cocktail Party)*.

Jedem das Seine

To each his own

DIE SPINNT JA!

German has many phrases expressing that somebody is nuts, a little crazy, off the rocker.

Here are a few that can be used in polite society. It is also good to know that in casual German personel pronouns like "*er*" and "*sie*" can be replaced by the definite article, like "*der*", "*dem*", "*die*" etc., and "*ja*" and "*wohl*" are often added for emphasis.

> *Der ist ja verrückt.*
> *Die hat einen Vogel.*
> *Bei dem piept's ja.*
> *Die ist wohl nicht ganz bei Trost.*
> *Der hat sie nicht mehr alle.*
> *Die hat nicht mehr alle Tassen im Schrank.*
> *Bei dem ist wohl eine Schraube locker.*
> My favorite, short and to the point: *Die spinnt!*

There is a wordless gesture Germans use: If someone looks at you and tips with his index finger on his forehead, he is telling you that you have a little bird inside your head, that you are a bird brain. Don't give this signal - also called the driver's salute - to a German policeman (*Polizist*). He takes it as "*Beamtenbeleidigung*" which means "insulting an officer of the state" and is punishable by law.

Now underline and learn your favorite phrase and use it when appropriate.

**Was man schwarz auf weiß besitzt,
kann man getrost nach Hause tragen.**
Johann Wolfgang von Goethe

**What you have black on white
you can take home with confidence.**

HEIM - HEIMAT - GEHEIMNIS

Heim rhymes with time. Its basic meaning is home. You say : *"Geh heim!* (Go home)" or *"Ich bin daheim.* (I am at home)".

Related words stir up deep emotions like *Heimweh* (homesickness) and *Heimat* (homeland, including landscape, culture, memories). Millions of Germans lost their *Heimat* in 1945 when they had to flee or were expelled from *Schlesien* (Silesia) , *Ostpreussen* (East Prussia), *Pommern* (Pommerania), and other areas east of the *Oder* and *Neisse* rivers which are now in Poland or Russia.

Some of the world's major troubles are rooted in some peoples' fight for their *Heimat*, see *Palestina/Israel*.

Strangely enough, *heim* is also in words like *geheim* (secretly), *das Geheimnis* (the secret), *Geheimdienst* (something like Secret Service or CIA), and *der Geheimagent* (secret agent).

To top it off, there is *heimlich*, which can mean homely as well as secretly, depending on context. But I hope there is nothing *unheimlich* about your *Heim* because *unheimlich* means awful, sinister, spooky. Yet we say *Unsere Lehrerin ist unheimlich nett* (Our teacher is awfully nice).

Glücklich ist, wer vergißt,
was nicht mehr zu ändern ist.

Happy is who can ignore
what can't be fixed - not any more.

VIEL GLÜCK!

Good luck charmes bring *viel Glück.*

If by the end of this year you have not received the good luck you deserved, you should consider starting the coming year with some of the charms that help the Germans in the Old Country:

a pig   (*ein Schwein*, like in *Ich habe Schwein gehabt* which means: I was lucky)

a chimneysweep   (*ein Schornsteinfeger* who still comes to your house in a black suit, often with a black top hat.

a toadstool   (*ein Fliegenpilz;* it has a red top with white dots)

a horseshoe   (*ein Hufeisen,* with the open end up so the luck doesn't fall out.

These symbols are used as New Year's party decoration and also worn as jewelry pendants.

The *Fliegenpilz* is so pretty, that a nice painting or photo of one can adorn your wall and nobody will know why you have it there.   I have a clay model in my garden *und ich habe immer viel Glück.*

Was du heute kannst besorgen,
das verschiebe nicht auf morgen.

What you can do today
do not put off until tomorrow

WIE GEHT'S?

The simple German verb "*gehen*" (to go) has so many idiomatic uses and meanings that it is worth learning some of them.

Try to match a number with a letter for the correct translation.

1. Das geht nicht.	a. He cheats on his wife.
2. Es geht gleich los.	b. I am doing fine.
3. Er geht fremd.	c. How does that work?
4. Das geht mich nichts an.	d. That won't work.
5. Der Kaktus geht ein.	e. When will the plane leave?
6. Es geht mir gut.	f. The clock is wrong.
7. Wie geht das?	g. How are you?
8. Wann geht die Maschine ab?	h. It'll begin soon.
9. Es geht um die Wurst.	i. That's none of my business
10.Die Uhr geht falsch.	k. The cactus is dying.
11.Wie geht's?	l. Now or never.

.

Lösungen:

a-3; b-6; c-7; d-1; e-8; f-10; g-11; h-2;
i-4; k-5; l-9

Geht das nicht einfach? (Isn't that easy?!)

Würden sind Bürden.

Great honors are heavy burdens.

ZUNGENBRECHER

Let's practice some German tongue-twisters.

Fischers Fritz fischt frische Fische. Frische Fische fischt Fischers Fritz.
Fisher's Fritz fishes fresh fish. Fresh fish fishes Fisher's Fritz.

Wir Wiener Waschweiber wollen weiße Wäsche waschen.
We Viennese wash women want to wash white laundry.

Wenn Max Wachsmasken mag, dann macht Max Wachsmasken.
When Max likes wax masks, then he makes wax masks.

Wenn mancher Mann wüsste, wer mancher Mann wär',
gäb' mancher Mann manchem Mann manchmal mehr Ehr'.
If some man knew who some man were, some man would give some man sometimes more respect.

The following version of *Fischers Fritz* is different from the one above. Can you find the difference?
Fischers Fritz frisst frische Fische. Frische Fische frisst Fischers Fritz.

**Besser ein Spatz in der Hand
als eine Taube auf dem Dach**

*A bird in the hand is better
than two in the bush.*

HERZLICHEN GLÜCKWUNSCH!

Here are are the most common ways to express your good wishes in German at different occasions:

Merry Christmas: *Fröhliche Weihnachten*!

Happy New year: *Ein Glückliches Neues Jahr*!

Happy Easter: *Frohe Ostern*!

Have a nice trip: *Gute Reise*!

Have Fun: *Viel Spaß*!

Happy Birthday: *Herzlichen Glückwunsch zum Geburtstag*!

If you want to mention the age of the congratulee, you simply write the number with a period behind it: *Herzlichen Glückwunsch zum 29. Geburtstag*!

To wish a sick person a good recovery: *Gute Besserung*!

To sign off on a letter or send greetings on a postcard: *Alles Liebe* (Love),

or

Herzliche Grüße,
  Helga

**Wer den Schaden hat,
braucht für den Spott nicht zu sorgen.**

*He who suffers the damage,
does not have to provide the sneers.*

IS A FRIEND *EIN FREUND?*

We often translate the word friend with *Freund*. However, they have different meanings within the cultural settings of the United States and Germany. In English I refer to hundreds of people as "my friends". In German I have few people I call *Freund* (or *Freundin* for a female).

Most of the folks I know are *gute Bekannte* (good acquaintances). To be a *Freund* involves commitment, loyalty, and usually common experiences in the past. "Buddy" might be a good translation in some cases.

German literature has through centuries glorified the virtues of *Freundschaft* (friendship). In Schiller's "Ode to Joy" (set to music by van Beethoven in his Ninth Symphony), you are invited to join in the jubilation if you are fortunate enough to be a friend's friend, *eines Freundes Freund zu sein*.

Of course, in the world of German teenagers and love, words take on a different nuance. When I was seventeen I answered *ja* when my aunt Johanna asked me: *"Hast du denn schon einen Freund?"*. She understood my *ja* to mean "Helga is seriously dating", and she advised me to leave school and learn something useful before entering motherhood - *Freund* as the committed boyfriend.

For 27 years, from the time aunt Johanna's boyfriend moved in with her, to the day she died, aunt Johanna referred to him as her *"Bekannter"*.

Andere Länder, andere Sitten

Different countries, different customs

THE STREET WALKER

Many visitors from abroad are reluctant users of dictionaries. They think they know it all and thus invite countless misunderstandings. My neighbor, for example, told me that his German cousin twice removed had very athletic children because they were all attending a "gymnasium" full time; he did not know that a "*Gymnasium*" in German is a school with college prep classes from grades five to thirteen.

On a visit to Germany, one of Austin's mayors wanted to cancel a speech on international commerce because in his final itinerary the word "*Hochschule*" (university) as the event's sponsor was translated as "highschool". His speech was not suited to that age group.

An elderly couple in our neigborhood invited their visiting German cousin Herbert to go fishing with them. "I go happy with", he said, "but you have ein angel for me?" After some snickering and whispering they promised him an angel. On the day of the trip a gorgeous blond divorcee joined them. She spoke German and found out that Herbert had not asked for an angel but for a fishing rod which, in German, is *die Angel*.

And then there is Else, who was determined to see a "Street Walker" before returning to Germany. I suggested a discrete stroll on Austin's South Congress Avenue where ladies of the night were rumored to be seen. Just in time Else's host figured out that all she wanted to see was a certain bird, the "road runner".

Eile mit Weile!

More haste less speed

SCH.....SH

The sh-sound - like in flash - is produced in German by three different combinations of letters:

sch (Busch)
st (s before *t* at the beginning of a word or syllable: *still*
sp(s before *p* at the beginning of a word or syllable: *spinnen*

Die Schwester spielt mit dem Bleistift.

Practice the sh-sound:

stumm - spielen - Schweden - Spanien - Stiefel - schwimmen - schreiben - Stammbaum - schlau - verstehen - versprechen - bestellen - einsteigen

And now, let's look at *die Wurst* (sausage). In high German you don't pronounce it "woorsht", because the *st* is at the end of a word, not at the beginning. Yet, you can speak with a bit of a southern dialect and say *,,Das ist doch Wurscht"* which means: It really doesn't matter one way or the other.

**Des Menschen Wille ist
sein Himmelreich.**

Man's will is his heaven.

ACH, DU LIEBER HIMMEL!

The German noun (*der*) *Himmel* has two translations in English: 1. heaven   2. sky.   That is an interesting theological and philosophical connection.

An overjoyed person is *"im siebten Himmel"*, wherever or whatever that is.

A warning to the speakers of German among you: When it's your time to go, make sure you go to the right *Himmel*. Otherwise you'll have to say: "*Ach, du lieber Himmel!"*, which means „Oh dear heavens!".

Gleich und gleich gesellt sich gern.

Birds of a feather flock together.

ICH VERGESSE NICHTS

German psychiatrists advise us not to use the negative statement: "Ich kann mich nicht erinnern." (I can't remember). We should be more positive like in:

Es fällt mir gleich wieder ein. (I'll think of it in a moment)
Es liegt mir auf der Zunge (It's on the tip of my tongue)

Instead of saying *Ich habe Ihren Namen vergessen* (I forgot your name) we should say:
Würden Sie bitte Ihren Namen für mich buchstabieren? (Would you please spell your name for me?)

Friends of mine recently moved to Sun City, a retirement community. Ever since, when they have a temporary lapse of memory, they say: "I am having a Sun City moment".

There is a very good and honest translation *(Übersetzung)* for that Sun City reference, however, *ich kann mich nicht dran erinnern, es fällt mir gleich wieder ein, es liegt mir auf der Zunge.*

Gut Ding will Weile haben.

A good thing wants to take its time.

SHE'LL BE COMING, HOLDRIO!

We remember a sentence in a foreign language easier when we sing it. The Langenscheidt company has published a book with useful German phrases set to familiar tunes. My favorite is sung to the melody of " She'll be coming 'round the mountain when she comes...:

Ich bin Ausländer und spreche nicht gut Deutsch.
Ich bin Ausländer und spreche nicht gut Deutsch.
Bitte sprechen Sie doch langsam.
Bitte sprechen Sie doch langsam.
Ich bin Ausländer und spreche nicht gut Deutsch.

It means: "I'm a foreigner and don't speak German well. Please do speak slowly."

Some of you insert a yippi-eh after when she comes. The German equivalent to this cowboy's yell is the German hunter's *holdrio* after *nicht gut Deutsch*:

Ich bin Ausländer und spreche nicht gut Deutsch, holdrio!....

After a trip to Germany one of my students reported that he remembered all the phrases he had learned as songs, but he had a hard time not to sing whe he used them in a conversation.

Why don't you try it, *holdrio*! ?

Wer wagt, gewinnt.

Nothing ventured, nothing gained.

WHAT IS A GIFT AMONG FRIENDS?

When a German warns you of a "*Gift*", don't take it lightly. "*Gift*" is the German word for "poison". Here is a numbered list of English looking German words and in a different order is a lettered list of their actual English translation.

Your assignment is to match the numbers with the letters.

1. BAD	A. RED
2. HOSE	B. GRAVE
3. WAND	C. BATH
4. HELL	D. NOVEL
5. NUN	E. TROUSERS
6. KIND	F. COTTAGE CHEESE
7. TAG	G. WALL
8. DIE	H. BRIGHT
9. TELLER	I.. CHILD
10 .NOT	J. (FLOWER) BED
11. HUT	K. WAS
12. GANG	L. DAY
13. ANGEL	M. HAT
14. GUT	N. FISHING ROD
15. RAT	O. WALKWAY
16. BALD	P. PLATE
17. BAGGER	Q. THE
18. GRAB	R. COUNSEL
19. ROMAN	S. GOOD
20. TOTE	T. SOON
21. QUARK	U. DREDGING MACHINE
22. WAR	V. NEED
23. BEET	W. DEAD ONES
24. ROT	X. NOW

Answers:
1 - C	2 - E	3 - G	4 - H
5 - X	6 - I	7 - L	8 - Q
9 - P	10 - V	11 - M	12 - O
13 - N	14 - S	15 - R	16 - T
17 - U	18 - B	19 - D	20 - W
21 - F	22 - K	23 - J	24 - A

Wie gewonnen, so zerronnen

Easy come, easy go

"MADE IN GERMANY"

German merchandise often displays the English words "Made in Germany". Why in English? The practice is based on a law passed in England in 1887 requiring all imports from Germany to be so marked. It was hoped that this would keep would-be purchasers from buying the items.

However, "Made in Germany" was soon regarded world-wide as an indication of superior workmanship and quality and thus was a boost to Germany's export.

I lived in Germany long enough to know that "Made in Germany" does not guarantee good quality, but it still evokes that expectation in many people.

How fortunate that the British required that the phrase had to be used in English, because in German - *In Deutschland hergestellt* - it might not have had the universal appeal.

Wohltun bringt Zinsen.

Good deeds bring rewards.

GIVE ME THE SPIEL

The German noun *Spiel (das Spiel)* has many meanings in English. Among them are:
1. play
2. game
3. gamble.

A *Spielbank* is not a bank for children with play money, it is a gambling casino, while a *Spielplatz* is a playground, and a *Fussballspiel* is a soccer game.

The verb "*spielen*" means to play and to gamble. In English we also use the word "spiel" to mean something like pitch. (She gave me the whole spiel on guild membership).

Spiel was probably schlepped into English from German via Yiddish.

Remember: In German the sp part of *Spiel* is pronounced shp, so the whole word is pronounced "shpeel".

Morgenstund'
hat Gold im Mund.

✦✦✦

The early bird catches the worm.

APOSTROPHES FOOL AROUND

One should expect the little apostrophe's function to be identical in English and German. Not so (*Pustekuchen*). "Ludwig's car" in English is "*Ludwigs Auto*" in German. No apostrophe, just an *s* added to the name. "Helga's corner" is "*Helgas Ecke*".

In old records and books you find several other endings indicating a possessive situation, like in "*Franzens Vater war Bürgermeister*". The son's name is not *Franzen*, but *Franz*.

In some old church records and other documents the Latin genetive endings are added to a German name or word like in *Christi Himmelfahrt* (Ascension of Christ).

German uses the apostrophe only to indicate that the vowel "*e*" is left out when the spoken language is reflected in writing. "*Wie geht's?*" stands for "*Wie geht es?*" "*Ich hab' die Nase voll*" (I have it up to here) stands for "*Ich habe die Nase voll*".

Of course, English has crawled into German, and now some Germans use the apostrophe like in English, especially in advertising.

Test for doing it correctly:
Who's corner is this? It is H_____ corner.
Wessen Ecke ist dies? Es ist H_____Ecke.

Frisch gewagt ist halb gewonnen.

❦❦❦

A courageous start is half the victory.

WHAT'S DAT?

What's dat? We know that German and English are linguistically related. Part of dat relationship is de fact dat many English words containing "th" have a "*d*" in German:

thin = *dünn*;   thick = *dick*;   thorn = *Dorn*;
thunder = *Donner*;   thistle = *Distel*.

north = *Nord*;   leather = *Leder*;   three = *drei*;
bath = *Bad*;   Heather = *Heide*

Can you find more th = *d* words in your dictionary or your memory?

By the way, what is the translation of "the"?

Papier ist geduldig.

Paper is tolerant.

INDEX ALERT!

Alphabetized indexes in German publications have changed. The other night I was looking for *München* in my new German road atlas and was startled: *Verflixt nochmal!* had they taken *München* off the map?

The *ü* used to he treated like a simple *u* for alphabetizing, and *München* used to be just below *Mummingen* in the index. After some searching I found *München* on top of the page well above *Muggensturm*. I realized then that the new German practice in indexing is to treat the *ü* as if it were spelled *ue*, although they still print it as *ü*.

This may turn out to be useful knowledge when you look for the name *Schütze* in the phone book on your next trip to the old country.

The same is true for *ä (ae)* and *ö (oe)* in indexes.

As if life and the German language weren't complicated enough without this new prӓctice!!

Wer den Pfennig nicht ehrt,
ist des Thalers nicht wert.

If you don't respect the Cent,
you don't deserve one Euro.

OI - OI - OI -

The "Euro" (*der Euro = 100 Cent)* has been the currency (*Währung*) of thirteen European countries since the beginning of 2002. It is important to know that in Germany one pronounces it "Oiro" and not "you row". *Eu* sounds like oi. *Deutschland* is "Doitshlund" and not Ditchland or Dutchland. *"Wieviele you rows kostet der Film?"* may not be understood by every German, neither in most other Euro-countries, because the only one where the natives speak English (sort of) is Ireland. Don't ask me how the Italians or Greeks pronounce the word.

Here are the countries in which you have to pay with Euro: *Deutschland, Österreich, Belgien, Spanien, Finnland, Frankreich, Griechenland, Irland, Italien, Luxemburg*, die *Niederlande, Portugal* and *der Vatikan.*

With all that simplification of currencies I expected all Euro coins (*Münzen)* to look alike, but *Pustekuchen!* (not so!). Each country proudly produces its own. Some coins minted in *Deutschland,* for example, feature the *Brandenburger Tor.* Do *die Griechen* sport *die Akropolis? Die Belgier* their *Männeken Piss? Was ist auf den Münzen vom Vatikan - der Papst?*

And how about Liechtenstein - should we expect a coin showing *"Der alte Herr von Liechtenstein"* dancing the polka around a beer barrel, *ja ja ja?*

Morgen ist wieder ein Tag.

Tomorrow is another day.

RISE AND *SCHEIN*

If you learn only one word today, you are earning your *Heiligenschein* (halo). As a noun the word is *der Schein*, as a verb it is *scheinen.* Both are homonyms, which means, they have a variety of meanings. There is *der Sonnenschein* (sunshine), der *Mondschein* (moonlight), and that glowing circle over your head, *der Heiligenschein. Die Sonne scheint* means The sun is shining. *Die Sterne scheinen hell über Texas* says The stars shine bright over Texas.

However, *ein Schein* can also be a certificate or a bank note. *Ein Führerschein* is a driver's license, *ein Hundertdollarschein* is a hundred dollar bill. Students earn *Scheine* for their courses to accumulate credits. To certify that you have donated all your earthly assets to the German-Texan Heritage Society, you ask for a *Bescheinigung.*

How paradox is it then that *scheinen* can also mean to give the appearance! *Der Ring scheint echtes Gold zu sein* means The ring seems to be real gold. We find the noun *Schein* in that sense in the often used phrase: *Der Schein trügt* (Appearance is deceiving).

By the way, that moonshine that your cousin's grandmother enjoyed was not called *Mondschein* but *schwarzgebrannter Fusel.*

Wer zuletzt lacht,
lacht am besten.

He who laughs last laughs longest.

IST DAS NORMAL?

Most English words ending in "al" are used in German with the same meaning (normal = *normal*). However, they are pronounced with the emphasis on the *al*, as if it were *normahl*.

Say the following words in German with the stress on the last syllable and guess what they mean:

international - formal - maximal - minimal - die Moral.
national - Hospital - Ist das nicht optimal?

Of course, they can have endings, but they keep the emphasis on the *"al"*:

der internationale Konflikt
optimales Wetter

Sometimes the meaning can be a little different in German:
To total a sum is *zusammenzählen.*
I totaled my car is *Ich habe an meinem Auto Totalschaden angerichtet.* (Considering the language problem, you'd better total your car in an English speaking country.)

Kleine Ursache - Große Wirkung

Big oaks from little acorns grow.

BIMBOS ARE *DEPPEN*

The pregnant chad - *das schwangere Papierrund*! It's history now, but for years to come we Americans will have to explain our presidential election of November/December 2000 to inquiring Germans. Here are the key words:

bimbos = *Deppen;*   butterfly = *Schmetterling;*
pregnant = *schwanger*;   chad = (I could not find it in any dictionary, but I heard it is called *Papierrund*);
ballot = *Wahlzettel*;   dimple = *Grübchen;*
lawyers = *Anwälte*;   to count = *zählen*;
to recount = *nochmal zählen*;   election = *Wahl*;
electoral college = *Wahlmänner*;   president = *Präsident*;
vice = *Laster;*   vice president = *Vizepräsident*

After I had explained the events in Florida to my German brother-in-law, he asked me: *"Wer war schwanger?"* (Who was pregnant?) I answered in desperation: *"Siebzehn Anwälte, ein Papierrund und zweihundert Deppen."* (seventeen lawyers, one chad and twohundred bimbos).

Kleider machen Leute.

✧✧✧

Clothes make the man.

DAS BAD CAN BE BAD

The English word "bad" is an adjective like in " I've bad news for you". The German word *"Bad"* (pronounced baht) means bath and is used in words like *Badezimmer* (a room with a bathtub). It also means spa like in *Bad Homburg* or *Bad Kissingen*, towns where people spend several weeks taking the "cure", *die Kur*.

With the *Kur* in most cases paid for by health insurance, *Kurgäste* (guests partaking in cure activities) have to drink evil smelling waters, be packed in mud, walk uphill, endure the sight of naked fellow patients in a sauna, and so on.

Doctors have hundreds of tortures they can prescribe. *Kurgäste* are to relax and recuperate from whatever ails them. Most *Bäder* (spas) offer groomed parks and outdoor concerts, cafes with sinfully tempting cakes, and afternoon teas with dancing. For these you try to win the favors of a *Kurschatten* (cure shadow), a person of the other sex with whom you spend relaxing hours of harmless flirting for the duration of the *Kur*.

Many spas feature a casino, a *Spielbank* with an elegant air, which attracts rich people, money launderers, the jet set and the international nobility. Among them are *Badenbaden and Wiesbaden*, with the word ...*bad* in the last part of the name.

I found a relationship between bad and *Bad* when I spent an evening in the *Spielbank* in *Bad Homburg*. I lost twelve Marks. And that was bad news.

**Wer nie sein Brot im Bette aß,
weiß nicht wie Krümel pieken.**

❧❧❧

**Who never ate his bread in bed
knows not how crumbs can prick you.**

WILL THE FLESH BE WILLING?

The German „*Peter will fischen*" does not mean „Peter will fish"; it means „Peter wants to fish".

The variations of the German „*will*" (*Ich will! Mein letzter Wille. Ich bin willig,* etc.) express a strong will to do something. Some quirk in the English language lets us use the same word „will" in "he is willing ..." as well as in "he will..." (as in "he is going to...").

So, when a German says: „*Ich will bezahlen*", don't assume that he will actually foot the bill. His flesh might say „*ich will*" while his spirit might be whispering: " I will not!" Or the other way around. If he means to say „I'll pay", he'll say „*Ich werde bezahlen* "or simply „*Ich bezahle.* "

For more information study the *Verben : wollen (ich will, du willst, ...* and *werden* as it is used to express the future.

**Wer sich auf seinen Lorbeeren ausruht,
trägt sie an der falschen Stelle.**

*He who rests on his laurels
wears them in the wrong place.*

GUTE FREUNDE

Good friends - how do you keep them? Language offers the perfect tool for cultural misunderstandings.

If it is said of a German politician that „*Er ist liberal*", it means that he believes in free enterprise, relatively free from government interference and support. Your German friend may have a good command of the English language, but he might still misunderstand you when you tell him where you stand concerning "liberals".

If a German tells you that he is „*evangelisch*", he is not part of an evangelical church American style. He is simply protestant - maybe Lutheran, maybe Calvinist, maybe a member of any number of Christian religions, but not a catholic.

It is also not wise to discuss taxes. The American income tax rate sounds so low to Germans in comparison to theirs. They get jealous. However, they don't know that we pay a lot of other taxes at a high rate - like property taxes - which they pay hardly worth mentioning.

Whatever you do, don't change the subject to cowboys and Indians. Germans tend to side with the Indians no matter what.

Zu viele Köche verderben den Brei.

❦❦❦

Too many cooks spoil the broth.

LET *VON* BE GONE.

"I should of went fishing" said my neighbor when he saw his mother-in-law pull into his driveway. How can the little word "of" be so badly out of place, I thought.

In most cases the English "of" is *von* in German, but in expressions of quantity it is simply not used:

a glass of milk	=	*ein Glas Milch*
a liter of gasoline	=	*ein Liter Benzin*
a bottle of olive oil	=	*eine Flasche Olivenöl*
a cup of tea	=	*eine Tasse Tee*
two cups of coffee	=	*zwei Tassen Kaffee*
a bar of chocolate	=	*eine Tafel Schokolade*
a bag of fleas	=	*ein Sack Flöhe*
a barrel of beer	=	*ein Fass Bier*
a glass of beer	=	_____
a bottle of wine	=	_____*Wein*

"That mother-in-law of mine really ain't so bad," continued my neighbor, "she's 220 pounds of love. How would you say that in German?"
"*Sie ist*", I said, "*zweihundert Pfund Liebe*. You couldn't of said anything nicer about her."

"Morgen, morgen und nicht heute,"
sagen alle faulen Leute.

✦✦✦

"T'morrow, t'morrow, not today,"
that's what lazy people say.

DAS MACHT NIX

The German word "*machen*" is related to the English "make", like in "*Du machst mich glücklich*". (You make me happy.) However, we often have to use other words to translate *machen*: "*Das macht nix(nichts)*" means "It doesn't matter".

Macht bitte diese Aufgabe: Welcher Buchstabe gehört zu welcher Zahl?
Please, do this assignment: Which letter belongs to which number?

1. *Mach schnell!*	a. Shut the door!
2. *Mach die Tür zu!*	b Take a photo of me.
3. *Mach die Augen auf!*	c. Turn off the light!
4. *Mach ein Foto von mir!*	d. Fritz is soiling his diapers
5. *Was macht ihr heute?*	e. Hurry up!
6. *Fritz macht in die Windeln.*	f. The museum closes at noon.
7. *Wir machen eine Reise.*	g. We're going on a trip.
8. *Er macht sich nichts draus.*	h. What are y'all doing today?
9. *Mach das Licht aus!*	i. He doesn't care for it.
10.*Das Museum macht um 12 Uhr mittags zu.*	j. Open your eyes!

Die richtigen Antworten: 1-e 2-a 3-j 4-b 5-h 6-d 7-g 8-i 9-c 10-f

Habt ihr alles richtig gemacht? Ja? Das macht mich glücklich!

**Gottes Mühlen mahlen langsam
aber sicher.**

*God's mills grind slowly
but surely.*

TAKE OUT THE MISSTERY

Is *ß* a mißtery to you? German has a letter which is always pronounced like the „ss" in Miss or the „c" in nice: „*ß*".

If you don't have the *ß* on your machinery, you can type ss instead: „*Strasse*" instead of „*Straße*".

The German name for the letter sounds like „esstsett". Sorry you asked? Many words with *ß* have a t in their English translation: *Straße* (street); *weiß* (white); *heiß* (hot); *Nuß* (nut); *Fuß* (foot); *Schuß* (shot).

And now comes confusing news: The new spelling rules - once they are accepted by everybody - will suggest that the *ß* is used only after a long vowel like in *Fuß* and after a diphtong like in *weiß,* but not after a short vowel like in *Nuss*.

To write: "I know that one eats the dumpling hot", one used to write:
Ich weiß. daß man den Kloß heiß ißt.
Now you write:
Ich weiß, dass man den Kloß heiß isst.

Nevertheleß, get a *Bleistift* and practiß: *ß ß ß ß ß*

Wer einmal lügt. dem glaubt man nicht,
und wenn er auch die
Wahrheit spricht.

❀❀❀

Once a liar, always a liar.

FALSCHE FREUNDE

Falsche Freunde are false friends.

Many words are similar in German and English, but beware of false friends: *„Gift"* means poison (*Opa gab Oma ein Gift* = Grandpa gave Grandma a poison). A *„Kommode"* is nothing to sit on - it's a chest of drawers.

When you are offered a *„Berliner"* for breakfast, your host is not suggesting cannibalism - he is offering you a donut of the kind my supermarket calls a "Bismarck". Kennedy was not a Bismarck.

A *„Kittchen"* is a slammer. *Opa ist im Kittchen* = Opa is in the slammer.

The American traveller with limited command of German really should have a printed list in German of *„falsche Freunde"* and learn them. Just like he should make a list of all the things he is allergic to and of the food he doesn't like.

Remember: *eine Angel* is not a female angel.

Wie man sich bettet, so liegt man.

*You've made your bed,
now you must lie on it.*

SAND IN MOTOR!

Learning means memorizing, and you and I need all the help we can get. Let's be grateful therefore for all the words that are the same in English and German, including the following:

Land, Sand, Ball, warm, Wind, West, Hotel, Bar, Auto, Restaurant, Start, Motor, Bus, Radio, Horn, Situation, Rose, Ring, Gold, Baby, Kindergarten, Statue, Vase, Arm, Hand, Finger, Pudding, Butter, Margarine, bitter, April, August, September, November, Podium, Bank, Tenor, Post, Tank, in, Gas, Marinade, Hamburger.

You can find more of the "same-words" in the dictionary.

It's fun to make up meaningful sentences in English using several of these German words in each sentence, like: The *Tenor* put his *Hand* in the *Pudding* and drank the *Marinade*, while the *Pastor*....(well, keep him close to the *Amen* and away from the *Gin*).

Wo man singt,
da lass dich ruhig nieder.

Where people sing you can sit down in peace.

IST ER BLAU?

You know, of course, that blue is *blau* in German, but that's true only when you talk about color.

When a German says *"Ich bin blau"*, he is telling you that he is drunk. However, when he says *"Ich mache Montag blau"*, he is telling you that he is not going to work on Monday, which may be related to our "blue Monday".

A very popular destination for a club's annual outing in Germany is *"die Fahrt ins Blaue"*, the trip into the blue. This means that nobody - except, it is hoped, for the organizers - knows the destination. Most of these mystery outings take place in June, especially on Ascension Day. Some clubs even hire a horse and a wagon from a brewery for the ride, and heaven only knows what libations the passengers endulge in.

Quite often some of the revellers return from the *Fahrt ins Blaue "total blau"*.

Jeder kehre vor seiner eigenen Tür!

❦❦❦

Everybody should sweep in front of
his own door.

THE FUSEDTOGETHERNOUNS:

There is no legal limit in German to the number of nouns you can string together to make one word. The limit is set by the intellectual capacity of the speaker.

The gender of a word like that is always the same as the gender of the last part of the fused word.

der Wein + die Flasche = die Weinflasche (the wine bottle).

die Flasche + der Wein = der Flaschenwein (wine that comes in a bottle)

das Leder + die Hand + die Tasche + der Preis = der Lederhandtaschenpreis (the price of a leather handbag).

The last word tells you what it is all about:
The often quoted *Donaudampfschifffahrtskapitän* is a captain *(Kapitän)*. What else do we know about him? He captains a steamboat on the Danube.

**Für jeden Topf findet sich
ein Deckel.**

There is a nut for every bolt.

WHEN YOU'VE GOT TO GO

"For gentle men only" said the sign on the door to the gents' toilet in the lobby of our hotel in Shiraz, Iran. Not everywhere do people try to accommodate the "English only" traveler.

"Toilet" or "Toilette", are words understood internationally, but not often used. If you are in need of public facilities in Germany, you might look for a big "*WC*" sign. lt stands for *Wasser Closett* (water toilet).

Other words for women and men are: *Frauen - Männer*; *sie - er* (she-he); *Eva - Adam*; and many more, including pictures and symbols to be interpreted at some risk. Then there is "*Herren*", which does not mean „Hers". but „Gentlemen". It goes with *"Damen"*, which means "ladies", dames or not.

In a private home you ask: "*Wo ist das Klosett (die Toilette, das Klo, das WC*)? Don't ask for the "*Badezimmer*" (bathroom), because that has a bathtub but not always a commode. How would you handle that?

In Portuguese the word is "sanitarios", and I whispered that word to our local tour guide in Brazil. He announced to the entire group: "You stay on the bus while I take Mrs. Helga to the sanitarium.

**Kümmere dich nicht um
ungelegte Eier.**

❀❀❀

**Don't cross your bridges
until you come to them.**

IN DIE SCHWEIZ ?

To complicate life, one has to use the definite article when talking about certain countries in German: Switzerland is *die Schweiz,* Turkey is *die Türkei,* Lebanon is *der Libanon,* and Iraq is *der Irak.*

We all know that *die* and *der* change to *des, dem, den, der, denen* and so forth if used in the genetive, dative, plural, or any other case. *Ich habe kein Bankkonto in der Schweiz. Amerikanische Soldaten sind in der Türkei stationiert. Beirut ist die Hauptstadt des Libanons.*

As far as *der Irak* is concerned, Germans had a problem in early 2003: not only did they have to decide whether or not to send troops there, they would have had to do it grammatically correct, of course. Headlines might then have read: *Deutsche Truppen marschieren in den (dem, der, des?) Irak* (German troops march into Iraq).

It's all so complicated *(kompliziert),* and it would be nice if we could just take a vacation *in der Schweiz* and not worry about *der, dem, des, den Irak.*

Der Apfel fällt nicht weit vom Stamm.

✿✿✿

Like father like son.

THE NEW SPELL ON SPELLING

It's hard to believe! Every few years a committee of so-called experts on spelling gets together in Germany and decides what official changes to make to German spelling rules.

Changes are based, it seems, on what mistakes are most often made and should therefore be made by everybody. The experts publish their judgement in a book called "*der Duden*", which is the authority on correct spelling.

The latest Duden has so many changes and (even worse) choices, that everybody is now condemned to be a pour and confuzed spella. The good old "*daß*" is now "*dass*"; the ace of hearts is now "das Herz Ass" (previously *As*)"; *die Spagettis*" have lost their h, but the coffee harvest has gained an e: "*Kaffeeernte*".

If you are suffering from rheumatism, you now have the choice between "Rheumatismus" and "Reumatismus". I prefer mine the old fashioned way with *Rh*.

Rast' ich, so rost' ich.

When I rest I rust.

YOU IDIOM!!

When I first set foot on American soil, an immigrant with limited grasp of English, I saw a man with a cart selling little sausages (*Würstchen*) that he advertised as "hot dogs". Horror! Shock! Nausea! Americans eat dog meat! They were even more uncivilized than their reputation. Had I not been penniless, I would have booked a return passage to Germany on the next boat.

My trouble was caused by misunderstanding an idiom, an expression that can - translated literally - scare a person witless.

Here are some examples. As you read them, imagine how they might be understood by a German:

1.virgin forest   2. great grandfather   3.midwife   4.German measles   5.horse radish   6.french fries   7.chicken fried steak 8. the dog's mistress   9.Excuse my French   10.They walk abreast   11.a black eye   12.She's in a jam   13.butterfly 14.Bottoms up!

Auf Deutsch: 1.Urwald   2.Urgroßvater   3.Hebamme 4.Röteln 5.Meerrettich   6.Pommes Frites   7.paniertes Rindsfilet in weißer Soße   8.Frauchen   9.Entschuldige den Ausdruck   10.Sie gehen nebeneinander   11.ein blaues Auge 12.Sie ist in der Klemme   13.Schmetterling Prost!

**Man soll das Eisen schmieden
solange es heiß ist.**

❦❦❦

Strike while the iron is hot.

THE UNDERTAKER AND THE FLYING SAUCER

"Under" is related to the German "*unter*". You can easily understand words like *Untergrundbahn* (underground train), *Unterseeboot* (submarine), *Unterhosen* (panties, briefs) and *Unterrock* (a lady's slip).

Then there is the *Untertasse*, which means "under-cup" and refers to the plate under the drinking cup: the saucer. That leads us to the flying saucers, "*die fliegenden Untertassen*".

"*Unterschreiben Sie bitte*" does not mean „Underwrite please"; it means "Please sign".

That enterprising young German who presents himself as an "*Unternehmer*" (literally translated that would be an "undertaker") is not an undertaker but an entrepreneur in an unspecified field, holding a highly respected place in society.

If one of your ancestors lived in Europe way back, he was most likely an "*Unterthan*", a subject of some king or prince, and therefore he had to be officially released from that relationship before he was given permission to emigrate. With that release he was no longer under the protection (*unter dem Schutz*) of the sovereign, and - on the other hand - your ancestor's foolish or criminal acts were no longer a blemish on the crown.

Alte Liebe rostet nicht.

An old flame never dies.

WANDERN

Mein Vater war ein Wandersmann, und mir liegt's auch im Blut.... Who hasn't learned that song as a child or in German class? *Wandern* (to hike) is a favorite and serious pastime of many Germans. Properly dressed for the occasion, often carrying a *Rucksack* (backpack), they cheerfully populate the paths in the mountains and the woods, the moorlands and the flats along the coast.

In the olden days a young man had to go *auf die Wanderschaft* and learn how his trade was carried out in different regions of the country. Only then could he call himself a *Geselle* (journeyman). From that period comes the wealth of *Wanderlieder* like *Das Wandern ist des Müllers Lust.....*

You can *wandern* for a day or for weeks at a time, stopping overnight in *Herbergen* (hostels), *Scheunen* (barns) or *Hotels* (hotels).

Wandern also means to migrate. *Der Auswanderer* is the emigrant, *der Einwanderer* is the immigrant.

Nursing frozen margaritas in the shade of a Texas Oak in July, my once-German friends and I dream about going on a *Wanderurlaub* (a hiking vacation) *im Schwarzwald* (in the Black Forest). *Auf, du junger Wandersmann, ...*

Ohne Fleiß kein Preis

Without diligence there's no reward

DELICIOUS *AMERICANER*

As a child I loved sinking my teeth into an *Amerikaner* (American). More about that later.

We use geographical terms to give names to items. You know of Hamburgers, Wieners and Frankfurters. However, the use of these terms can lead to misunderstandings. When a German offers you an *Engländer* (Englishman), he is talking about an adjustable wrench, an item we all need when travelling. When it's Greek to you, it is *Böhmische Dörfer* (Bohemian villages) to the German. A *Nassauer* sponges on other people. John takes coal to Newcastle, Hans carries *Eulen nach Athen* (owls to Athens). When Americans say Let's go Dutch, the Germans have no clue to what that means. The very concept does not feel proper to them, and if they agree to it, they might say "*Jeder bezahlt seine eigene Rechnung*".

A *Römer* (Roman) is a long-stem wine glas, a *Pariser* is a condom, and a *Berliner* is a certain kind of a doughnut, also known here as Bismarck. Kennedy was no *Bismarck.*

The delicious *Amerikaner* is something between a cookie and a poundcake, but you can't buy it any longer by that name because the name became a victim of political correctness, I was told, along with the word for my beloved *Negerküsse* (negro kisses), which are chocolate covered marshmallows.

Politics in a German pastry shop *(Konditorei)* !

Was man nicht im Kopfe hat,
muss man in den Beinen haben.

✵✵✵

What you didn't do with your head,
you have to do with your legs.

DIE NACHT BEFORE CHRISTMAS

A German-English Version of Clement C. Moore's
The Night Before Christmas.
by Helga von Schweinitz

's war die Nacht before Christmas, und all durch das Haus
Keine creature sich muckste, nicht mal eine Maus.
Die Socken were hung by the Schornstein mit care
In der Hoffnung that Nikolaus soon would be there.
Die Kinder were kuschelt gar snug in their beds
While Träume von Zuckerplums danced in their heads.
Und Mama in her Häubchen und ich in my Käppi
Had g'rad nesteld down für a long Winter's nappy
Als out auf dem Rasen such Getöse arose,
Ich sprang aus dem Bett to see: Was ist da los?
Away an das Fenster ich flog wie ein Blitz,
Tore offen den Laden, the sash just a Schlitz.
Der Mond auf der Brust of the new fallen snow
Gab ein Glitzern of Mittag to the Dinge below.
Als, was to my staunenden eyes should appear,
but a Miniatur-Schlitten und acht kleine reindeer,
Mit 'nem Kutscher so lebhaft, so alt und so klein,
Ich wusste sofort: das muss Nikolaus sein!
Und schneller als Adler, his coursers, sie kamen,
Und er pfiff, und er schrie, und er rief sie bei Namen:
"Nun, Däscher! Nun Tänzer! Nun Pränzer und Vixen!
Auf, Komet! Auf Kupid! Auf, Donner und Blitzen!
To the top of the Vorbau, to the top of the wall!
Nun eilet euch! Eilt euch! Eilt euch, y' all!"
Wie trockene Blätter, die vorm hurricane fleuchen,
Wenn sie meet mit a Hindernis, zum Himmel hoch kreuchen,
So up auf das Hausdach die Tiere, they flew
Mit 'nem Schlitten voll Spielzeug und Nikolaus, too.

Und dann in a twinkling hört' ich auf dem roof
Das prawning und pawning of each kleinem Huf.
Als ich drew in my Kopf und was turning herum,
Down the Schornstein kam Nikolaus mit 'nem Klumbum.
He was dressed ganz in Pelz von his Kopf to his Fuss,
Und his Kleidung war tarnished mit Asche und Russ.
Ein Bündel von Spielzeug war flung on his back,
Er sah aus wie ein Händler , just opening his pack.
Seine Augen, wie sie glitzerten! Seine Grübchen, wie merry!
His Bäckchen wie Rosen, sein Näschen wie a cherry!
His drolliges Mündchen war drawn up wie a bow,
Und der Bart on his Kinn war so weiss wie der snow.
Den Stumpf seiner Pfeife hielt er fest in his teeth
Und der Rauch, der umkreiste den Kopf wie ein wreath.
He had a breites Gesicht und a rund little belly
That shook wenn er lachte, wie 'ne Schüssel voll jelly.
Er war chubby und rundlich, ein recht lustiges Elfchen,
Und ich lachte, wenn I saw him, in spite of myselfchen.
Ein Zwinkern des Auges, und a twist of his head
Bald gab mir zu wissen, ich had gar nichts to dread.
Er sprach nicht ein Wort, ging direkt to his work
Und füllte die Socken, then turned mit a jerk,
And laying his Finger aside of his nose,
Und giving a Nicken, durch den Schornstein he rose.
Er sprang auf den Schlitten, to his team gab a whistle,
Und vondannen sie flogen wie der Flaum einer Distel.
But ich hörte ihn rufen als er drove out of sight:
"Eine fröhliche Weihnacht, y'all! Und Good Night!"

Ende gut, alles gut

All's well that ends well.